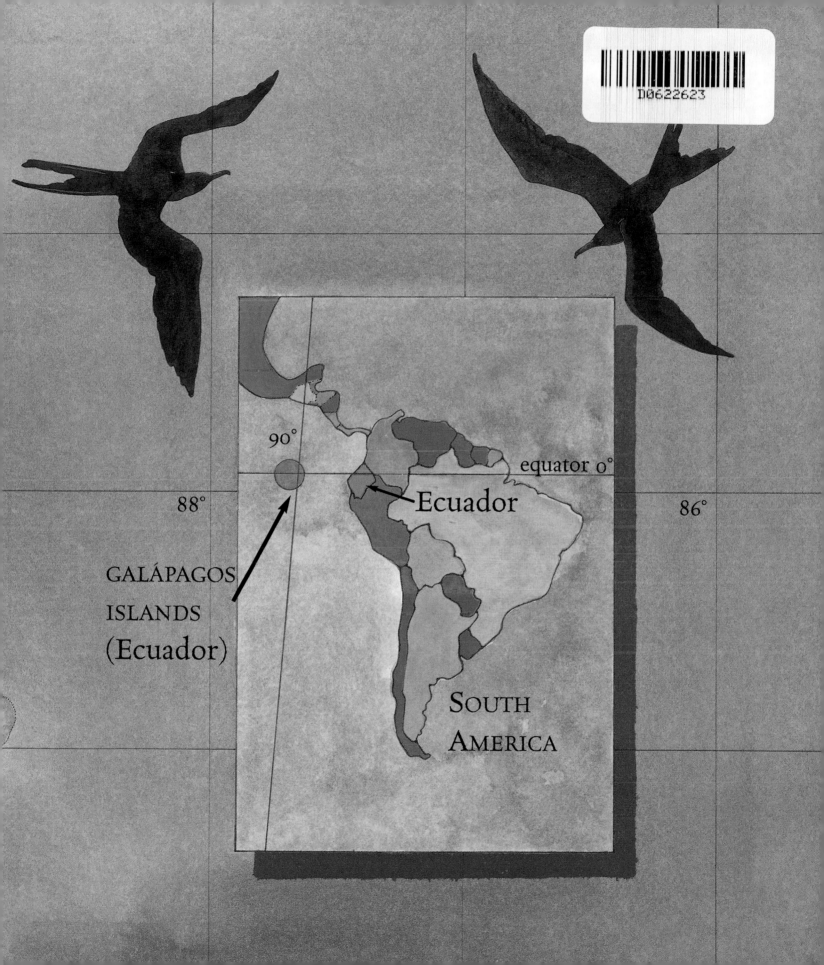

D0622623

90°

equator 0°

88°

Ecuador

86°

GALÁPAGOS
ISLANDS
(Ecuador)

SOUTH
AMERICA

Lonesome George the Giant Tortoise

Francine Jacobs

Illustrations by
Jean Cassels

Walker & Company
New York

The sun rises over Pinta Island in the Galápagos. A giant tortoise creeps out from under a bush. He is longer than a yardstick and weighs almost 200 pounds. He is all alone, and his name is Lonesome George.

Tortoises are land turtles. They never go into the sea. George's shell rises in front like a horse's saddle, so tortoises like George are called saddlebacks. Their shell's high opening lets them stretch their neck to nibble on tall bushes.

George warms himself in the sun. Soon he is hungry.
Tortoises have no teeth, so they use sharp ridges on their
jaws to bite plants.

A prickly pear cactus pad, covered with sharp spines,
lies on the ground. *Chomp! Chomp!* George has his
breakfast, eating the whole juicy pad, spines and all. He
gets the moisture he needs from cactus pads, grasses, and
other plants because there is no fresh water on Pinta
Island except for the puddles that form after rain.

George raises his head and looks around. He sees giant cactuses and silvery trees. He raises his head still higher. Something is coming his way. It's another tortoise. Maybe it's a female. George wants to mate. He can't have any little tortoises alone. But the other tortoise turns out to be a male like him. Better luck next time, George!

The sun is overhead. It's too hot for George, so he settles down under a shady bush for a nap. Tortoises are reptiles. They need the sun's heat to give them energy, but they also need shade to cool down.

When George wakes up, it's cooler. Small brown birds pop out of the grass and strut in front of him. They are ground finches. George knows just what to do. He stands up and stretches his legs and neck. Finches hop onto George's legs. One jumps onto his neck. George stands perfectly still. *Peck! Peck! Peck!* The birds pick seeds and tiny ticks from George's wrinkly skin. They clean his face, eating the pesky insects.

The sun is low in the sky now. George moves on. There's not another tortoise in sight. George comes to some thick brush. He burrows in until he's snug. He tucks his head and legs into his shell and goes to sleep before the cool night comes.

The next morning George is out on the hillside again. He spends his day eating and napping. Sea lions snooze on the sandy beach below him. Black marine iguanas and bright red crabs cling to rocks at the water's edge. These animals all mate and have young. George has searched and searched, but still he can't find a mate. Female tortoises are nowhere to be found on Pinta Island.

One day a fisherman brings three goats to Pinta, so he and other fishermen can eat fresh meat. The goats multiply. Soon there are four, then a dozen, then a hundred. Before long, goats are everywhere. They eat the grass, the shrubs, the cactus trees. They eat everything!

George and the other tortoises must climb Pinta's steep slopes to search for food. The higher ground is dangerous. Behind thick clumps of grass lie deep holes and wide cracks. Tortoises tumble in and can't climb out. But George is lucky. He stays safe. The trapped tortoises die, leaving George more alone than ever.

One day George crawls over a loose stone. Uh-oh! He slips. He tumbles over. *Crash! Bang!* George lands on his back. He is in trouble! Unless he rights himself, he'll die. He stretches his long, leathery neck and pushes his head hard against the ground. He rocks from side to side. *Whap! Whap! Whap!* Finally George manages to roll over.

Years pass. The goats on Pinta Island continue to multiply. The three become 30,000! They have almost stripped the island bare. With little to eat, the few tortoises left disappear. But George survives.

Wardens from the Galápagos National Park want to save the island's plants. They come to Pinta to shoot the goats.

The wardens discover George while he's resting in the shade of a tree. They mistake him for a goat and almost shoot him. But, just in time, they see that he's a giant tortoise. They are amazed to find a giant tortoise still alive on Pinta Island.

The wardens want to protect George, so they will take him to the Charles Darwin Research Station on the island of Santa Cruz.

To move George, the men tie him to a makeshift hammock. It's hard even for strong men to carry a giant tortoise down a rocky mountainside. George has never been off the ground before. But he survives the trip, and the wardens put George on a boat to the research station.

George's new home is a big pen inside a wall of lava rocks. Grass, bushes, and cactuses grow there. Workers make the pen much like Pinta Island. They hope George will feel at home. Keepers bring George lots of papaya fruit and grass. They can only guess his age. They think that he's more than sixty years old. That's not too old for giant tortoises. They can live 150 years or longer!

News about George gets around fast. Newspapers say he's the last of his kind. They call him "the loneliest creature on Earth." The keepers begin calling him "Lonesome George." Soon people all over the world are talking about Lonesome George, the giant tortoise. Visitors come to see him.

Wardens search Pinta Island, but no female is found. A $10,000 reward is offered to zoos and collectors for a female tortoise from Pinta. Some zoos have saddleback tortoises, but no one knows if any are from Pinta Island.

It is feared that when George dies, Pinta tortoises will disappear forever. So scientists put two female tortoises from a nearby island in George's pen. But George ignores them. He seems to want a mate only from Pinta. The wardens have rid Pinta of goats. The plants have grown back. Finding a tortoise now in all the brush will be much more difficult.

Scientists haven't given up trying to find George a mate. They have developed a new test that can tell one kind of tortoise from another. They will use it to search zoos around the world for a Pinta female.

With luck, George won't be lonesome anymore.

About Giant Tortoises

When Spanish explorers came to the islands and saw the shells of the giant tortoises, they called these distinctive reptiles galápago, which means "saddle" in Spanish. As a result, the species came to be known as "saddlebacks," and the islands came to be called the Galápagos. The Galápagos lie in the Pacific Ocean, 600 miles west of Ecuador, the South American country to which they belong.

The Galápagos tortoises are the biggest tortoises in the world. Two basic types live on the islands. The smaller ones are saddlebacks, like Lonesome George. They have long necks and shells that are arched upward in front. These traits enable them to reach higher in search of food on dry islands. The larger ones are known as domes. Their shells look like upside-down bowls. Some domes weigh as much as 600 pounds and have shells more than four feet across. Domes are grazers and live on islands where plants are plentiful and within easy reach.

Years ago pirates, whalers, sealers, and others took thousands of tortoises from Pinta and other Galápagos Islands. Many were females caught nesting in the lowlands. The hunters carried the tortoises off to their ships to be eaten. Then collectors came and took still more tortoises away to museums and zoos. To make matters worse, rats and cats came ashore from ships and ate young tortoises. Then settlers arrived with farm animals: cattle, pigs, horses, donkeys, goats, and dogs. Many of these animals fled into the wild. They ate the plants that tortoises need for food. They trampled tortoise nests, ate eggs, and killed hatchlings. Few females were left to bear young, so giant tortoises grew scarce. The government of Ecuador has laws to protect giant tortoises now.

Lonesome George has lived at the Darwin Station since 1972. Thousands of people have visited him there. You can visit him too or see him and other giant tortoises in videos and movies of the Galápagos.

For more information about Lonesome George and other giant tortoises, write to:

The Charles Darwin Research Station
Puerto Ayora, Santa Cruz Island
Galápagos, Ecuador
South America

Friends of Galápagos
Charles Darwin Foundation, Inc.
407 North Washington Street, Suite 105
Falls Church, VA 22046

or check them out on-line:
www.darwinfoundation.org
and
www.galapagos.org

The author at the Charles Darwin Research Station

To Ben, with love. —F. J.

To all those working to preserve the Galápagos and their unique place in our world. —J. C.

Special thanks to Dr. Peter C. H. Pritchard, director of the Chelonian Research Institute.

Text copyright © 2003 by Francine Jacobs
Illustrations copyright © 2003 by Jean Cassels

All rights reserved. No part of this book may be reproduced or
transmitted in any form or by any means, electronic or mechanical, including
photocopying, recording, or by any information storage and retrieval system,
without permission in writing from the Publisher.

First published in the United States of America in 2003
by Walker Publishing Company, Inc.

Published simultaneously in Canada by Fitzhenry and Whiteside, Markham,
Ontario L3R 4T8

For information about permission to reproduce selections from
this book, write to Permissions, Walker & Company, 435 Hudson Street,
New York, New York 10014

Library of Congress Cataloging-in-Publication Data

Jacobs, Francine.
Lonesome George, the giant tortoise / Francine Jacobs ; illustrations by Jean Cassels.
p. cm.
Summary: Describes the life of Lonesome George, the last living Pinta Island giant
tortoise, from his search for food on the Galapagos island to his days at the Charles
Darwin Research Station, where scientists are encouraging him to mate.
ISBN 0-8027-8864-5 (hc) — ISBN 0-8027-8865-3 (rein)
1. Lonesome George (Tortoise)—Juvenile literature. 2. Galapagos tortoise—Juvenile
literature. [1. Lonesome George (Tortoise) 2. Galapagos tortoise. 3. Turtles. 4. Endangered
species.] I. Cassels, Jean, ill. II. Title.

QL666.C584 J33 2003
597.92'46—dc21
2002038073

The artist used gouache on 140-lb. Arches hot press 100-percent rag
watercolor paper to create the illustrations for this book.

Book design by Diane Hobbing of Snap-Haus Graphics

Visit Walker & Company's Web site at www.walkeryoungreaders.com

Printed in Hong Kong

2 4 6 8 10 9 7 5 3 1

GALÁPAGOS ISLANDS

Pinta

Marchena

Genovesa

0°

92°

91°

90°

8

Fernandina

San
Salvador

Pinzon

San
Cristóbal

Santa
Cruz

Charles Darwin Research Station

Isabela

Santa Fe

1°

Tortuga

Santa
María

Española

Pacific Ocean

2